colonycollapse
metaphor

Cover image: photograph of Tanja Miljevic by Ralf Rodriguez

Cover and book design by Joel Craig

Published in the United States by Fence Books,
Science Library, 320 University at Albany,
1400 Washington Avenue, Albany, NY 12222

www.fenceportal.org

Fence Books are printed in Canada by The Prolific Group
and distributed by Small Press Distribution and Consortium Book
Sales and Distribution.

Library of Congress Cataloguing in Publication Data

Jencks, Philip [1963 -]

Colony Collapse Metaphor/Philip Jencks

Library of Congress Control Number: 2013932324

ISBN 13: 978-1-934200-74-2

FIRST EDITION
10 9 8 7 6 5 4 3 2

Fence Books are published in partnership with the University at
Albany and the New York State Writers Institute, and with help
from the New York State Council on the Arts and the National
Endowment for the Arts.

To join the Fence Trust, contact editor Rebecca Wolff at

rebeccafence@gmail.com.

Fence Books
Albany, NY

colony

metaphor

Acknowledgements

Thank you to the editors of the following publications, in
which some of these poems appeared:

*The Canary, Chicago Review, The Cultural Society, Drag
City, Effing, Fence, GutCult, H_NGM_N, Information
Booth, Mary, MoonLit, Poetry Foundation and Chicago
Printer's Guild, Rabbit Light Movies, Traverse Journal:
Robert Duncan Tribute Edition, Typo, Venereal Kittens*

Some of these poems first appeared in the chapbook
How Many of You are You by Dusie Press (2007).

Dedication

I owe infinities of gratitude to so many, especially the following people. In many cases, without them I would not exist. Additionally, many have assisted me tremendously with the process of bringing the book together. To Geno Foster, Kirby Haltom, and Michael Newton. I love you. I will never forget you. May you rest in a better place now. To my students, Mike, Carrie Olivia Adams, Ghada Albeheary, Rabbi Batsheva Appel (KAM Isaiah Israel Congregation), Rabbi Herbert Berger (Beth El Synagogue Congregation), Ares, Rob Arnold, Zach Barocas, Rabbi Berger, Lauren Bianchi, Ray Bianchi, Paul Edward Blackburn, Susan Bordo, Daniel Borzutsky, Julia Cohen, Joel Craig, Grace Dillon, Sarah Dodson, Loretta Downs, Drag City, Joshua Edwards, Eric P. Elshtain, Richard Every, everyone at FENCE, Angela Foster, Ben Friedlander, Geoffrey Gatza, Jonathan Goodman, Laura Goldstein, everyone at H&L, Neil Michael Hagerty, Kevin Holden, The Howling Hex, my mother Denda Jenks, my father Alan Jenks, my sisters Elizabeth and Rebecca Jenks, nephews Zane and Avery, Devin Johnston, Jamie Kazay, Kaetlin Kennedy, Kevin Killian, Yves Labissiere, Robbie Lee, Andy Macleod, Karyna McGlynn, Christopher Mattison, Jenny Mayfield, Sebastian Migda, Tanja Miljevic, Josh Miller, Simone Muench, Rian Murphy, Oscar, Osiris, Michael O'Leary, Peter O'Leary, Walt Pearson, Herb Reid, Ariana Reines, Jessie Richardson, Ralf Rodriguez, Tim Rutilli, Fred Sasaki, Larry Sawyer, Jen Scappettone, Robyn Schiff, Mike Signs, Matina Stamakakis, Elizabeth Treadwell, Nick Twemlow, Lina Ramona Vitkauskas, Rebecca Wolff, and to survivors everywhere for your strength and courage.

Table of Contents

hives

Let Fridays decide
Our fate tho
There be no such
Thing as
Fate or date,

Bus stop y
Travel hex
Sits in city planners'
critical of a land
without bugs.

So it's a wire crossing.
Hatchet hatch
Does splits, "behaves"
Let Fridays decide
Hives
And recondite
Remonstration,
Self to self turns.

Let nothing or no one
Take the place of
That fundament
Iterate the gristle.

Kicks and kids
Venerate the treasure
Chest organs
Dissect or standby
Weapon in purchase
In chase in rats

In veritable

Crash

Let Fridays decide our fate.
This one will do me in –
I know it. Care about it.
Being done, this Casket.
Without One Question
But becoming One.
Sap or Venom,
Depend on Who You Ask.

• • •

I dreamt we were on this ship made of bone
Speaking a language I've never known.
a retrieved memory of that which has never happened,
happened. The mast and prow were all tusk
and we grafted to it. Underneath the deck
Jimmy said he asked God for grace but drew mercy instead
But it came out all garbally toothless cab driver palsy.
We had music too for a while, bone and waveform
Imprinted on the night with something endless
Lurching over us until we landed in the morning.

burial

Ice on an ice cave.
I guessed you knew that.
Done thought thinks you was been a mind reader or
Thinks that the limit inside itself
Murders the word with electrical shock.
Suicide solidifies in a soaked uncrushed mandible
I'd like to be an alley cat's meal —

When the world is done with me done with me.
A real wave to the animal, what is an arm hi hello.
Chest rafters and skulked invented teeth that
needle these unprevented streets, this little
limb of mine for I'm gonna let it shine let it
Shined. Incautious to glare of unrefuted
refracted telegraph phosphorescence.

Scalps what is human it guessed the alps.
From the fire an escaped look at you eating
what i ate. An intestinal love, our first love
last to admit, but then gristle half grins all got
visceral the way the bodies mime traffic in decay.

Topers

What is integrity?
And the null
Bumping against it,
Dumbly, automatic
Like teeth grind the night
Away. Sleeping, but not.

What is integrity?
Integral to Being and Non
Needs it to. Integrity
Integrates the two.
It's always doing
Those things behind my back.

I lack it for asking,
Says who? I am sure I heard
That voice
But no one is here.

It copies nothing.
Never pokes holes at ekstatic.
What is? v What up?
In a crowd, the latter wins
Out, with a right hook
On Being and Non-Being.

Once, there was a climbing
Perambulance revelating topers
Vents of horror
With little hot hotels
Flashing lights beam

flick morse code.
It was integral to understand
The message
But the fierce flashing killed everyone
In the building.
One, in conversation, in love,
Living fully measured,
Looked up and started
To seize . . .
This guy was reading about
It on 34th and Belmont,
Outside smoking, tapping
his left index finger
it made little insects
hiss & snicker.

Abyssal

Abyssal. Some amphibians'
Retinas will only respond to motion.
Carnal, carnival, carnivore
Woods were carved out
When they walked . . .
"plank"
Weekly inveterate bruising
Just in time for what
You were having,
Low, lower
Artifice of accidental instinct
Or accretes "intentions,"
Bested beast.

Anthem

For David Grubbs and Susan Howe

Thread of sparrow blood
Snowy flag spiral to eidic oath
Tent city 13th century, few live through.
Flocks of geese, before
What is Canada?
observe camp
elegiac unheard song.
Fluttering fief,
Finding cover always underneath.

"decides"

They moved me.
Skull babies with
Their tricks of fire.
Ohm, this is the light.
Ohm, a black and
A white television.
hmm, is the little
Bits of prince.
Duke of the chamber.
Fitful follicle
Election of elecution.
A ball hinged, permeable.
Hips respond to other hips,
Vocable of the insides

．．．

you cannot leave the subject blank
you said you were in Madrid
but were not. the bot
checked on you recursively
reclined in Beaverton.
Tons of the smallest animals.
their certitude of motion
underfoot. this when you
look down, is what we call ground.

canst tho du?
kanne nicht.

unbounded bleacht needle
streets where the unbleached
go to get their washing done.
(There's that ton again.
Almost like a city.)

you arc and pull back
from fragment
from firl
marked manument
testemoney et tu
other patrimonies.

you got screwed by lunar
eclipse calculations
in the back of your neck.
when he beckoned you
forget the incisions
that were made,

eclipse chips restorative
justice ceremony. moneyed
lips and criticisms shipped
by jocular gerunds, fun
fundamental garage gatekeeper.
"daddy long legs"
"it's a preying mantis (no it's not)"

lurches worse than that there
church with fires flickering
forced the pit people into
dynamitted cabinets reticulated
with rustic conundrums.
with or without lipstick,
but this one kind you must halve.

Halva was free for every
religious occasion. Someone's gotta
finish the wine. Uh oh operation
won and there's convulsions
flipperant and opera
of ghastly armeries.
soldiers climbed up
civil war trees to amsterdam
this one out, but we hung up
a whole set of photos,
skeleton surveillance
"MRI" courses in veins,
in white outs. "venison for cats."
slick immoderate venerate
vertebrae, sores and stasis.
put me back up there,
this place is dkilling mesa.

• • •

We forget ourselves
Parking lots full of it -
Playtime plots engrave a name.
When because of you and also you
A drenching thanks and praise
Vivifies the void quietly quit the
Security State. Jesus, we had the other half covered
But the afterthought
Exposed the afterflesh of Christ
Who crystallized the quiver
With trembling arrows.
"will not be worsted" (Psalm 127).
Kids get sorry for the exposure
Make up stories
That cohabit
What lies between us.

• • •

My pinhole weighs a ton.
Said it was Gospel to legible
Letters. Darkling legions

Of molecule, peril inscrutable
Missing matter. They'd have heads
On platters if _____ made it legal.

"it's sufficiently vague so the dead
are historically portable" What's
that? Heard some nothing spinning ahead

There is the opposite of what just was,
Which isn't to say you aren't now,
You are — but up ahead is

Your inverted afterthought. Think how
Like destiny already skulks.
Made in and out of metal coal dusted towns

Tons and tongues of rasp, stalks
Of maize, beatings, auction block
Blocked from memory, outlined in chalk.

Myopic

hung up
your calling is waiting.
you were just discussing
the metaphor, how dreams
run aside one another
and the attendant problems
of answering when they cross
over.

every other sign is against you,
facing. mute. either reluctant
obedient or "taking a chance,"
praise the perpendicular.
see sun redding the sign, this
time from thirty feet.
it won't last.
it's a gas.

∧∧∧

I thought we had our gas lessons.
Wilfred Owen masks and the whole
green lens blowback Dulce crisis.
Shoah. Gulf. And, respectfully, friends
and colleagues, thought that
if I tried to do as Celan did
or Stanford
or name your favorite death-trip,
that would be to say
to gas myself in the blasting
beautiful blue light of the day
smokes alone, porchly — even delight,

to gas and gas and gas
o but only myself,
so is ok
but
you see
meine friends there
is a problem. I only exist
at intersection. This is why
you never see me alone and
tiny fascist invisible retroactive
compels at the lonely, "another lonely."
in grammar, font, styles. lifetimes of the.
as you may see it would not be good poetry comma
but only the forgetting. perhaps a footnote to a conference
without recompense, without embrace, without chance
and a Dugway Proving Ground stance, atomized
and worthlessly alone
which I'm not period.

• • •

Ashamement. State or stasis, also stasi.
Is n ot the undertone any
More thane it is the tone of
This precision crows me to your bones.
We précis and precious offerings
Maybe this year's a tulip on that especial
Occasion to maker your marker,
You know the glib remarks
Demand a recount with
The other faces.
And fortunate
For you
Every
Other
Face has
Benn melted
Away with fear
And time and travel
And o those years you
Outlasted them all so take
Comfort kick up your feet on
The grave right next to you and
"Die" laughing. You will notice as
You heave into the morning hours
That I have shaved my head in observation
Of your untimely and horrid and horrible death.
It's just that you call it something else and don't knowtice.

• • •

What's the temperature of a god?
Implacable invertebrate noses
Through fences.
This is the time of the fever.
If so, the ovens need no explanation.

God hovered over, guarding.
Provisional
Sacrifice, slaughter,
The sader's dead.

"drink four cups
And call me in eight
American days"

Love,

YWH

• • •

Airport security checkpoint absolutions,
Wave the magnetic wand
Across your body,
Those red laser trinities
Transmit across the sky
To someone different than you
Or me, elegiac uncertainty
To prove that which isn't
Holds the new holy ghost
Caughts in gasps, ingests.
X-ray courtesy assistance,
O please take off your
Shoes and climb through
To the other side.

Typists Versus Printers

the typed word is what
isn't on the page.
It is literally   off the mark
(that's some fanciful musing
you might say.) No, not some
talk of this exceeding that.
It's just that typing
and prints are different,
as citizen to government.
And pages are full,
except by typing removed —
as groves plowed to farms,
under threat of Storm.
All that is needed to be said
or done is,
by pages in stages
save for a day when
word may interrupt
and blow the world away.

• • •

Who wants to be a damaged cowboy?
maybe desert or range;
picked apart of what once was started
Only to be finished again.

His Johnny Walker eyes
Didn't even flinch
At his own disappearance
Only to reappear on stilts

Still suited for the road tho
The haunt of every "rest area"
Here's my favorite cabin captain
Blowjob trees and rest stop amputees.

Compatibility Mode, Diagnosis

Neurotonic clonic Klonapin
Remeron rememories
Or depakotastica.
Sports Clean room envy . . . .

Some grass and beside of it
A choosing. Allergic to's
Set that next to a war
And carve out a casket.
It all full of you "head full
Of snow," y packet of bloodshot
Brutes to go orders
Shrapnel pick up sticks
And glue bag parades
Made a brut trinket
a medicinal delicate.

• • •

So it's inside itself
Has wherewithal to stand
Bello be belong,
As is also bees
Whose frenzy
Is mistaken for a buzz.

Catalytic. It got to run
After you, when you
Refracted back in between innings
For what ere approacheth
Cirrhotic gauze and all
Shimmy shine or felt up
Under bleachers
For what worth
The end of pharmacy soda.

oops e all gummy,
flips with y wait unt.
Lacerate sense organs
Chime glib mr tambourine
Jangle chicken man,
Pooched and ribby,
Has fun in the sun.
Roman rivulets
Copurse through you
Tell, telephone, Teller Ede.

Who blames Jane Fonda for a heart attack
Due to her protests about Three Mile Island?
Hoofy. It's a glue problem again,
Huff, hooves, gelatin,
And the melted you out in Nevada
Nervy Athens,
Polis poles apart.

Mechanics do it
to each other.

Hydra Reads A Lancet Report

Alt, Altamont and bruise
Venerate is venal,
Empathic or deviltalk.

It's not that you,
Or is, is. On impact
Exploring artifact
Resource management,
File under bullet mænldʒmənt.

That's not cerebral really,
It's just brains and metal
Mixed together.
Hot weather for it.
Scorch orange darken wet sands
Push 700,000 by New Year's Day, 2007.

Dr. Tea Stain
Pipes Beggar's Banquet
In Kirkuk headphone, he's in his heaven.

(Really, Hydra mutter
it's time to hang
the President for what he done. Redacted text.
NSA parenthetic paranoia purposeful
Somnolent slang.
Nosey little noose.
See him and his men
Strung out on bacilli and spirochete,
Duncanly or Operation Whitecoat.
What did they do to the Seventh Day Adventists?)

A Count

I.

For if he were to have any
of this, it would make him sick
not from lack of supplication
but the bent forms that find
themselves in the drink itself.

Such a custom, as by habit
and cunning we end completely.
Capitulate.

II.

Very form. Its very form.
for if he were to learn of any
of it, the learned themselves
they make themselves sick in it.

This endowment of angles
would that we were in gear
and could drive away
as at that one part of the
movie where every character
ceases.

III.

Course legend.
He would die of custom,
himself sick,
in gear,
a movie character
ceasing.

IV.

I told you not to.
I warmed against it.
And even as you became
the act, it was cunning
of you to capitulate,
the gas fumes or these
heavy cousins whose
heft of heart
cleft lip banker plus dowdy wife
doodle up a storm
but do not drink of it.

V.

To not do it,
as in every relation
this venerable opposite.
My venereal cousin's
lips cannot speak and
I cannot speak.
Don't tell me of Volcanos
and this or that eruption
from your infected neck.
Use the one that talked
me into this earlier
when we were staging.

this one is tiny.
I'll send you a seven by morning
but will be of course late
for it. If you tell me you're tired
one more time, I'll get sicker
too just to upstage you
mine will be more intents
a little carnival
to shave points
off the balance sheet that's
been inveighed for so long
I've lost count.

I will count this one thoroughly
I will douse this one
by air, a flyover
"crop duster"
a cought citizen
that mine will be the one
that he might drink
and be sick of it.

● ● ●

I think I should like a thing
for its stable inalterable Occupation.
and yet, there are such guilty things
as deficit and want may trumpet.
And shines.

I think I should like to shine
then and only, that this may be
the time when we could.
you, me, and the things
emulate each others' presence.

And anticipates
are things too.
with ghastly energy
I think I should like a thing
and anticipates are things
too.

That should flag a thing,
to look back on it
and all that it occupies
that breathy unalterable
archival gullibility.
I keep with Sound.
And anticipates are things too.

• • •

that should mock a thing.
as a channel or freight
which cannot but ring
its own declension.

or gut — to cradle or reverse
this, the yarn and that,
Jacob's Ladder.
He tried to sister and sing

but it was of no clatter,
and was left aping
his own half-baked memoirs
or I forget. Something about charm

or school and the kids.
Let's put masks on them
and fill with sugar, hon.
that should rake a thing.

I thing in sister declension,
but cannot ring
because I'm aping yarn
in sade clatter, it's all sugar
and they saw me
on the corner frequently
adjusting my mask
that alternately frightens
or enlarges the sky
that's baked black
with gouged glints
flaked across it.
You can't see the Ladder
or climb out

because the pinholes
in your plastic cover face
are so tinsel and reticent,
that's okay that's okay.
The school daisy with her
collectible elf army,
and vestibule will watch over you.
As Countenance collects
her little dimpled dirty.

To pain a thing, which you
discover on the third day
at the third rail, fetching glimpses
of the light from your jailhouse
choir. Each of them, a mask to
fit the stories they expanded
over drinks that one night.
everything is heavy from
the chainroom. With its crashed
purple disastrous sunsplit
enclouded monument to
time. Which should not count,
but does only and exactly
that until you special little
face etches you to the task
we have so considerately
assigned you, from the corner
of the morning, when you were
trying to dream we put the chips
in and you thought it was
a loud and soulless alarm
or train.

the way you shook.
we took pictures of you too,

with the garden chairs
and daisies to boot.
to gouge a thing
just in case
it might sing
and remind
us which songs
you grew up to.
which would date you.
which, of course, is the only
date you'll get after a certain
number of years on this dirtball
hurling at the sun
without preface or index.
You've been fitted for this fine day,
a sort of retrograde graduation
a poofed out tongue
"more face to wash"
it's a look we cannot put
a finger on, but the choir
made for you a song,
off Journey's Infinity
about the lights and the city
and you see, isn't it shitty
to know every note
in a non-retro way.
You may exit to another speck
on the Dirtball
but the wrecks of you and what
you done done are engrooved
on your pattering and delicate
grainy face. To cover it with hair
in the off chaince we won't recognize
anytime that you want me.

Isolate

what chance for what was

now castigate.

not the hour

but what counts.

a bath?

or his entrusted belt.

even the petunias

may listen briefly

or glanced at,

thought beyond thinking.

Who, what roots?

Books crease everything.

Bracelets gleam their gamble.

The attached to

Eyelash cursive

dusty coordinates

drew upon, unaware.

much later,

doused in morning

liquor.

• • •

crosses and fingers.
cute shoots and bloody ladders
master of the bladder
of the life of the mary.
got scared one at a time
look at this he said to me
it was not a head talking
he picked up but
antennae. no not radio,
that would be a disaster
with all the channels,
this one made of harbors
and meat clung to bones.
i lived in the leftovers
behind the barbeque
in hot nights for you
covered in it. in shit.
that's the whole ego thing agin
back there is where the
fetuses were kept too
famous little secret medical spot,
so it was political life
we was living, boned and less so,
mutes glaring at each other
in mounds please someone stick
around because the way that
one man makes them talk with
their chinny chin is wrong.
he turn it into song,
breaketh ankles
with little Altamounts.
They are talking to each other on the inside

flipped bandages and soul food "half racks" cozy dives
smokes packed in there.
chinny chin chin,
a little teapot, chin chin
in spoutless offering them legs
and grin. cant talk to you
or you to me, someone
rigged the restaurant
clinic made to order
a round godless hot mess
play the organ loud
"chest fever"
stitched in my neighbors
dumpster psalm 139
james version.
we are mutes using wire signals
we strap them to ourselves
and goes the hot night
impounded Allah
please call the restaurant
first even a blood let
notes to get the children
out, thank you very much
that explains the whole dumpster
thing patriarch tradition
conditional uncondition
traitor psalms and he
sees what is going on.
He is the first and last voyeur
looks at that melted chin,
predetermined or determined,
chin up.

• • •

smoke on the porch
an infinite span of finite land.
bee devils buzz and huzz
beneath your quarters,
flaring out — yellow and black
the becoming blue sky —
"Water Tower." and birds and birds
sing sing span of wings differences
disappear at this hour.
huzz of the Queen buzz.
Her desolation and infinite grace?

Come out and hear see
before the blasted sun rises
Come out and hear see
before I can see you,
covered in animal, gunting
all the shovels and all the ditches
the "necessary"
hunches at every skyline balks
to put the bees away and be waking
Being, only. bark and
these eerie leaves huss the wind
will verb you. "Cabrini Green"
uh-oh. They sought to spread us
out where we could not hear her
but only see. Of a certain Order.
The Empire's stench tucked
into Fulton Market, pig and fish
guts splayed in hot art district.
Or tricked out on 95th and State.

span of wings differences
disappear at this hour.
gut check gouged by Time
come out before the disassembly
line tears into heart
this muted belief
that we could be

Irascible Tenant

seroquel. ardent neural raid.
irascible tenant,
"you are incorrigible, simply incorrigible."
reflections of a dying paper route.
or was it boy. that was my intention
when he was bested at the helm,
when he was blankets by daylight
and mouthing sections of biblic'
portion, oozing at mandible.
Take a certain someone, add gun
and some radiation. "treat street."
the Hatchers had one under couch
for special haunts. He grips dripping
without days without number, just
characteristics denoted
without sail, without border, dead
time circling, circling (ah) del'very!

• • •

Each day tears the heart apart.
Which god can serve as suture,
To stitch together ("I feel the same
Way about disco as I do about herpes")
Fumbles fools for food
Interval tube
But the mosaic is flush with agape
Proves to itself its own emblematic
flesh the food is written in.
flesh of you on flesh of the world
your body's hand regulated by
eruptions of where it reaches,
it touches branches,
cannot stitch or e.

Rearrange for vital strategy sessions
Put together the gap with matchsticks
To map
A false witness which one will
You pick — made up by choices
Multiplying upon each other
"Hummer" "Garden"
The finest wine grown from
The wettest mouth a garden
God little Dionysian money fucker
God of dissolution, is no gap
Between what is you and you.
Plainly folded sheets
Over tidy folds of blood
The morning comes all over your bed,
makes a son collect his debts
From the shriveled bodies
Of his southern family.

The body "gone south" —
This one is all meth.
It is not the needle itself
Which dulls and bulges
To tighten the skin against
The possibility of sleep
So there are no gaps.
Daynight stop eating,
But rather the needles
That come from up under
The skin and poke themselves
Out from within, "heebie jeebies"
Or "creepy crawls"
Remind you of what is real?
Eventual manifest of the bugs
plant in your body,
Garden gone loco
Obliterate ill literate
Lances. Locomotives jab
Jealous of what is fixed.
This is why every train
Needs a track.

I'm sick of experience,
Stupid little ante.
Comic cut ups of morning
Glower at each other
Over office game brackets.
I want the god of the unopened,
Tradeless, fuckless
Who never sleeps nor wakes
Dissipates nothing.
This God is Flesh Itself, entirely.

november

something there is that loves
an arrow, or flattery like
when the current
or blaming mouths
in mirrors to private
discernment and alarms

engorge every room's
crease. you can't hear
how you sound

and the voice in your
head plus the ones that
surge. nothing can muffle it,
but everything shows up
instead.

Notice first.
groove in couch
or tore up face.

house no food
and he show up
on the third day,
shut in and announcing.
He shuffle some promise
which is just enough
to stave off
an evening out
taking cell pics
of yourself and all

those who meant so
much, who you can no
longer detect
save for screen
reflections and the outpost
toilet scene because
you agree with yourself
that it must be a case
of November.

• • •

And that's me over there by the dandelions
Oppositionally, a man wears a gigantic hat
Plummets into the bins for bottles and cans,
Things that are returnable show up in the morning.

I contend to my weed friends that we show up
Everywhere, growth inimitable trajectories
You won't look up but I love you just the same
As if you were God, as you are.

Cracky pavement pushes you into the world.
A scientist came and measured the length of
Each duration, for life; takes notes to watch us die.
Once he recorded the ecstatic explanation,

When he played it back, everything you said or did
Ran down into the hole, backwards. Even the stars
Possessed with the dark ran down
Into it, each one a mole with a little secret,
Burning burrows underground.

Seventh

from the seventh (0) o our heads o will rock o cute cut courtesy class
classy classroom claims. form of claimant on the seventh form from the
sixth head for what was dead for who was spent for who went dead
inside for who walked cuts and all this lite litany bebom bemoan no
window for you are such stung such hung form not trying sedition. THe
edge of his thick arm bulched in mischief (no relief of soul in this song,
white on white paint tight wound protestant tumor, that you-weren't-
born-rightness of it cusps i(n gutn ribs gouged for frolick mowed downy
before the down, back at the blown animal parts gnashing his
confederate anyotherway glutted howls r holds proud that gun I do not
know the type for the / am backing up out of the store it's not because
of

I'd make a sound for the form of the store in which he hevered.
and clews found not the taxidermied deer head or cigarette pouch of
flesh,
but

from the seventh great monument to the Confederate Richmond
complicit citizens silence of free thinking maybe a little march to march
against the marchers, seven forms of seven fields damages crutched in
naked shocked in underground richmond shackled prisoner he a comin
verse is a dreamin jammed in seven bug meals jackals in his skull will
joke this is the last supper he speak with them compartmentalized he
laughs cuz they turn into flies batting around what was his waist.

from the Seven Confederate

for sixteen temes he did gorge and raste.
his tensils founded on haggard hate

crosst with machine gun from wall hung
with several others and three discrete caledars
brushes for 1.35 other sundry items.
Spent by the rich and sum of us who sneer at the animal
beg severed sickly and stuck up, hoisted man monument
destruction et cetera. yesera. And also this other side
unseen glass eyed we missed the animal we hunted
down and gunted, fisted and monkeyed, classified and regimented
aug and demented. verified and confederized so it's not human.
he's no person or he is and as such is lesser.
which is our war but that deer on the wall be proof
of his wretched and gunly and gassing qualities.
in the lens you see he may double read as Nazi. (or Shellac)

Shellacked in raw curves.
so there was a river where he hung his horsey noose
and delivered fateful blow to her so he would know
with the widest of eyes. And, he thought since a horse is a captive then
in this sensee he would experience the double feeling of captive murder
hostage harem confederate reenactment mothafucka gonna go down he
halls angel dave or something dragged it all across the shimmeri
rocks and i could tell you how he cried and these were different from
the horsey teaers that happened earlier so they were split. in this, he
was rich. so full of fuck.
and encrusted with hate. thing is, there's a wander alone in when they
go fishin
for it. singular target aim. fixed and focus. dragging the river since youre
gone plays the radio.
hum. it's not hard to understand. unlimited limited laminated river drag.
(thnk we got sum . . .)
they share lots but everyone's got their own cap encrusted with the
skull's detritus history.
and little nixon buttons stuck straight into skin to prove the mark.
things y6ou know nothing about. it's the moment before the
assassination and we gather at the river with confederates to decide.

there's talk of jobs and something of a fight in Oakland, as shadow. Since it is also 1968 in 2009, then everything makes a particular sense. You could say that it isn't 1968, and you would be correct. you would be correct. you would be so right. how right you are. you are so endeavored and accurate. Your brilliant acumen and mathematical precisions not to mention sense of historical nuance reflects a great capacity to rote it all down. now if you'll excuse us . . . .

●

Cutting Hegel

where did I go.
rake or varnish,
to. it wasn't in you
the doing otherwise.
verification takes time,
killing time,
splendid — in the way
that immolation
refigures itself
not the delegation of
time as in
factory to spacecraft.)

no.

these are other smokes.
see how you cinder
the
holocaust
did not end.
can not.

this time, you also
must put yourself
into it. It's your
responsibility.
an ethics of reason
slices birds in shreds
in flocs.
damaged flagrant pilgrim
mutable force march.

it's not march.

did see cuts on hear t
monastic encounter.
put yourself into it.
this is your job.
you're great at it.

II>

here let's cut Hegel in half
and just stick to synthesis.
it's going to have the lucidity
of things at a distance the way
presidents may appear presidential,
you seem certain at this level.

plus it makes something new,
which is cool too
your pallid frame undulating
coursing river blood rushing
to every part and no possessive
apostrophic moments everything's
dotted with creation.
in this limited sense, I rationalize
our fucking as resistance to
hegemonic monads.
but this is what kills me.
spent limit skin dissolution
wet winsome boy bar dance
it's inimitable the way your lip
curves at this particular moment.

the idea of the child versus birthing.
aliens verb the body
bordering immigration
police the alien and
it becomes the police.
refuse and
God will slit your
throat down at the bottom
of this most privileged and
well executed armor
just to test
if you have
the resolve
to go nuclear.

Poem after Hart Crane's "Paraphrase"

In the broken staring seat inside
Retina, vitreosity waves-in-the-tide
We crashing to this key in synch
Have bound this vision, etched out our time.

Beneath the belly the crafted cloth
Is bound into those decibels of want:
In what finds off beside unfolds the fold,
Invokes in blushes, at commingling stance.

How in their moment! When will the eye see,
For perpetual orbs will eventual(ly) flank
The dream — how intermittent is the sleep
That can not knot — as quick the song's collapse

When, if tossed by this amazing blast,
Your eyes, hypnotize in a trance, by now
Filled with us, write the bright signature
Beneath broken scribbles in the hidden hall.

Dear Jason

I just got back from Vermont
Herd there ws a poet up there
When you walk in the moonlight
Something else is happening
Like when they let the idea of it
Bob up from undur water.
Gasps I want to see you
Then down for the count.
Van sent his garden and regards
the nation state torn apart
Shorn I guess they let it up
For long enough so over in the
Hanging tree someone inverted,
His shadow got told to the door
And his pardon, floors all.
Made a little hiccup with a trinket
At the throat of it thick and thicketed
Massive mixtures of red and pomp
Something no one could any longer
Defend there was a fly before the
Fly fisherman said some somnolent
Inherent Herr, mercurial herring
Someone fed the cats mercury, unwittingly
Because they ate the infested fish.
O dear Jason I wasn't a good geologian
And couldn't believe that lottery
When the cats came to they were cliff leaping,
What this looked like to the village
Every poison had a reason so they said
But Charlie nature took a leap that day
And came to the river's poison floors
I got all jittery and wisht the invert

Shadow state Hobbesld monster
Stript and stripper, dead blues monster
Gript and giffy with Pride
Prickles his needle armor

poem for neil

of the way the bats
smell you can
miss seeing them
cave.

when she said
bats are like rats
i say no,
they are inverted swallows
dives in not at
what is hollow.

a hollow is not hollow either
got mud and guns,
it's not a steeple but
chasm pull and push
all us little people.

no, I said peephole
isn't empty
necessarily, fills
with spies and nixon grins.
slides up next to slither
absent the ability of site
can always listen.

I will "tell us more about my first painting" I will I will. I will tuss about
and tell us more and more and more. I will I told you I would and I did
and you want more how dare you wanting wantingand then not wanting
and in your not wanting also do I construct a wanting. I tell you more
theree is snakes and planets and profiles and horizons and moon o yes
there is that and there is cruelties and wars and flesh and there are
quotes from friends i mean this guy makes enemies not in the mean
sense but they are "made up" (like lipstick on my vomit spings and
sprung versies) i will tell all alal and alla. I tell Jesus andJessico undun for
you for you i clipt a glance of her in the corner it was a wrapped
body that would not move, then it was two, then on the third month in
the 7th year it was three. that seven th year was three bodies alla that
year. little Eggs snapping at them for even for warps and for gods all
smeared and tired of Gost stories inculating geist sanedi this is not some
king lear shit and it isn't any other lear he said f you for saying it might
be for being all holier than tho about that s__t and then talking talking
with your little p p friends in the bak of things when you thot no one
could see hear you cuz you is privy. we hoisted up wine from the cellar n
i was too scared to eat the bred i told you because i believed the dream
with its "lady this is my sonnet" except in this one there were seven lines
and everything was cut in half ("Oh the Streets of Rome are filled
with...")

"I'm proud that I was able to start with nothing, plan it, and have it work as perfectly as it did . . . . I sleep clearly every night." (Paul Warfield Tibbets, Jr.)

1985: "Iraq had been one of the few countries independently invested in women's education."

<u>*Lesley Stahl on U.S. sanctions against Iraq*</u>: *We have heard that a half million children have died. I mean, that's more children than died in Hiroshima. And, you know, is the price worth it?*

<u>*Secretary of State Madeleine Albright*</u>: *I think this is a very hard choice, but the price--we think the price is worth it.*

—60 Minutes, May 12, 1996.

Each of us here as divinely as any is here. *—Walt Whitman, Salut Au Monde*

Eichmann thanks Madeleine. Passes in Olympic Fascion. Trophozoites trump babies. triumphal geno moment. liquefied populace, once reading amazing books we have magick turn learning to bloodfilled shit. turning the arc of a lover's gesture to blood filled shit. price calculation: rigid rational. magic logic, does math in millions and blood filled shit. In the name of Jesus Christ our personal Savior and family vengeance. some can more readily accept the end game. humans liquid. dechlorinated waters. watery babay. more accustomed to witness body piles than decrescendo of smaller decays. did family first guess flu? a gurgle in the eyes, only moms would recognize? no perception of town yet. She look at her eyes, instant obvious wrong. What did we do last night? Swift change of diet. Give the child more water. (name them all! each and every. Madeleine learned it best not to use numbers in this calculation. To liquefy astrology, she inverted her earth sign. Zodiac. Preserved in Baghdad, Damascus. ruled by Aldabaran, "the Follower." On January 8, she tells Kofi please keep up the WMD thing after Jan. 20, 2001. Weapons of Mass Destruction sung by administrations sounds like JesusChristmypersonalsavior it's said so fast and rhythmic, systematic state mantra.) What little gesture, perhaps a jig or smile in particular touch

reaches beyond signature. *Salut au Monde's* postscript. little and bigger
animals too. some correspondence gives a clue to the wretched fact.
notice of mucous and blood-filled shit. this time, no one gets a number.
runs in rivers. Albright Nixon Eichmann séance. Let's summon Warfield
Tibbets: "We think the price is worth it." no cooks in the
kitchen kuchen. the tape's recording but on erase. pardon the cliché, but
this one's a new globalized smallpox blanket. specimen daze. liquefy
you, whoever you are. I blood filled shit, indiscriminately,
discriminately. Apollo sent a crow to get som waters. beked buket of
Hydra brought back. poisoned blood of Hydra. go fetch. kids in streets. a
little hydra in each. with every mother's effort and stitch, each sacred
child churns blood filled shit.

gargantuan reading projects
sunburnt boys must wear
the lit tle hats at the regional
party. Tulsa vs. Morgantown.
"BBQ Baloney"
"he was called Madsimmeon,
yet he was not insane.
('Let us drink!')"
cartoon pools
th rotted flesh
this is a quiet one.
we can dance to it.
this is not a falling apart off point.
bloat of time. so we cough more
often, everyone's grown up.
kep growing an there's no move
to room around. sno tear carpets.
donning the most historic of hats
I'm skirting Vietnam on Greco
shorelines. coinhabited
ghost: a bevy of gassed soldiers,

skinny stryngs drag femurs
in jangle. some navel whistling.
To pretend the Orphic.
avenging insult to the Father,
 we gave dysentery to this
citizenry in smallpox pilgrim
nostalgia.

• • •

you did not become animal, was. thanks for the body w/out organs,
omg. awesome! your adjectives were as antibiotic some
septic to strip through being, at the crosshairs,
chiasmic. "I don't believe that/s" selft self-effacing
selfhood, hooded by your own insistences on an ownership
to exist through its nonexistence. Proclaiming. Reversing
and then claiming again. The BWO is nowhere better. is not
Nowhere either. Didn't you notice the language always
announced your appearance, yet always qualifying itself
that it might efface the very selfsame thing it always Erected?
And there was venom, hideous, blazing and biblic
inside the inside where there is nothing but
goblin chattering with Golem. Inside the freezer,
burned by thousands of efforts to perfect the structure
around it, encasing it, verifying its own "to-be-looked-at-ness"
emphatically not, for the facticity of pores, scores of them
and the slices of brain that intersect: to make eyes that see
and a certain repeated posture of lying. Plus the problem of holes.
The whole mouth problem uncompresses your desituated unverifiable
verities. It's the crucible, really. That radical disjuncture
of your letter and your name, of type and rallying cry,
and the sad aping of memory mistaken for prescience
what springs forth, a horrified being proclaims itself
self. It would be the mis-take of the most marked margin
to call you liar. There is nothing inconsistent about you.
Everything about you has its consistency. One of utter body hate
detailing itself over and over again, repeatedly washing
at the shores of some truth river or something. Introjected,
maybe this time the trip inside won't unleash that most
terrified and cruelly malformed being, but a becoming with.
never and always this will come to be. never and always
because you refuse the angle at which language turns the body
inside out and what that means when one hand slides upon the other.

• • •

Mysterium Tremendum

For Rabbi Berger, Beth El Synagogue, Durham North Carolina

Bess was my gussy friend
She always took care.
From the friction
Or could. a bell is something different.

Altogether. Scuh costly errors
Of the mind. Eso and exoterror
Skeletons. The pink body
Eating its shell.

She had pleaded not to pick
Up with the underneath
Legs and all scrabbling.
But the fluorescent tests
Allowed for prepreception.

Every ghost limb has a war story.
But not every war story has a limb.
Fifteen thousand candles are
Little kittens. It's an exed out eye
Thing for this one.
Or in the rubble, an Oboe
Tuned by the wind.
Half of him is impounded
In the tree folk
Gemeinschaft
Half of him is a city.
If you call him in the forest
You might get the gut side
Vertiginous and quiver,
Covered in vines and hair
To camouflage

What's on the inside that counts?

What fixed and determinate story
Hails from the forest these
Fisted halls?
Most of him is hanging in the tree you
See blinking in the sunlight, such a drip.
The rainwaiter tickles the private.

Got to get it together.
From formal folk
Comes the shining.

• • •

gutful prolapse on the dancefloor.
aka sorry fred no boot worth getting knifed over.
strung up on a string to catch a thing
and feed it upwards, anchored versus kiting.
and the whole freedom question
which gets us back to the knife/boot space drama.

I stopped gutting things
which incidentally were not.
Guess that the agents had me forgot
Andele scrubbed off the floors
to hide the prints of where we had not
fought.

Cliff swore up and down he saw
her in the knife glister pattern,
Never could trust him, tensiled jawbow
ever since he stitched himself
up as his own hero an I had to
lay him down and talk him into
turning himself in for the shooting.
O man as Sarah might later say . . .

• • •

For Rian Murphey

Morgantown, West Virginia. earth smell of pauper's graveyard. Engulft
codeine coff syrup drinks over unitown disco snuck in strange cocaine
in twelve year old brayne. Eating mom's Hadassah lox late in the night.
Didn't tell you but the one time you left town without us it was an
allnight party then me and Heather drove to Chicago to see Rian
because Rian is Rian. Pawns daddy's boom box in Indiana. The
"mountaineers" saying allnight party is redundant, unless it's Saturday
in which insert tailgate. Decides Robert fripp is god I will cut my hair
like Robertfripp and disappeared all the king crimson cassettes under
my one good arm the other, had been jumped dislocates shoulder 25th
wedding anniversary needs consent for repair of arm liz me and becca
fell apart the same year. 1978/79. when police came this time I returned
most of the cassettes but kept one copy of each. Dad gives otto, process
theology, church and renderings of mysterium tremendum under
renderings of mr tambourine man. Also we go to synagogue sometimes.
Mitzvahs, the significance of

1930

Black minds. Efforts were made to build, encaged.
Works Progress Administration develop
Sick White Magic. Engraved, segregated.
Second Ward (a) Negro Elementary
Also grab it known as "Annex." Invasion.
Lady Eleanor she show up she herself
Dedicate the Segregated surgery
On the 1925 dilapidate
Dilate the pupils
"New Deal"
White Avenue.

*

"Everyone looks the same in a coal mine."
Utopian impulse, intensions bested by accretion
Of time. The same old new deal,
"other half" and have-nots.
Can't tell slavery slant.

*

1973

Tangled in the bramble,
On the corner of Posten and White Avenue.
Integrated Annex.
The rooms filled with dozens of decibels,
Mostly white.
Honest, I had no idea
But our hilly tangle
Playing field gave some pause.
In 1973, we debated whether
The new merry go round was
Giant tit or flying saucer.
Call it what you will
I imagined it would spin me
To somewheres bettersafer.
Mamaverse.

(What happen in the bathroom?)

Philosophy

Well well well oh well (John Lennon and the Plastic Ono Band)

As the well is a ditch with source up in it.
Hey, Come up from the you can never see the
Underground Railroad from here. The retroact-
ive survives in metallic temporal lobe.
Bears witness. The subway, Personal Rapid
Transport System, great endangered greyhounds.
Sacred and scared trains and tracks compact or
Complicate, it is place that does not change. The trees
Survive. Witness, please slit your luck in travel.
This is no pulling a geographic as
The astrologer cult folk salesmen say. But
Rather, an articulate arc shooting up
from ditches. Light of mine, light of the mine.
A black crescent from the underground dusted,
Determined, scintillates — scathing backwoods
Glance. Glacial shifts tectonic. What is freedom?

Bats

How many of you are you?
I told you, you should see where I was sitting
To see the show.
This is it, sunlit, straps, nest, and bottle.
Apocryphal window,
But oh it certainly is true.
"And Also You" watches the Power Plant
Consumes poison for the venom of dawn.
Protect Nature charged with ions
Enfolds with flood of bats.
I left some food for you to share
In a white container to the far right.
Encircle and become left.
There's a mattress to crash on too,
Blotted with sun and one question:
How many of you are you?

Kill You Power Plant, Begins at Acts 2:1-13

The screen is the place where you go to watch the show.
This is how sum of it all goes down it's a
desperate movie, really. Upsample
flower power monumental,
"Kill You Power Plant". WVU.
"Jan 15" which is MLK
Or the dimming afterimage
Of what you thought might happen after
It didn't, burned into bridges
The seats are all gristle, mattress and bottle.
You should see where I'm sitting to take this one
For you (awwwwww).
Buildings wedge hills for screening room,
Blaring sirens backmask soundtracks
That crash the shore of the edifice.
Gritty Decker's Creek overpass that Mistah Bee jumped from
exiled on his bicycle. I would skip a thousand kickball
Games for one phrase of his mad beautiful Black Jesus sentence
That trailed off the bridgely artifice
Spright and buggy, smeary glasses, his old school bike
Punctuated by the now bloody brown crik.
Before the time of the screen or even built bridge,
Bonehead crept across the lower beam, "protect nature".

Ballroom romper room

This is where they play Who Are You? Real loud
I was watching Zoom. Puts "the needle and the damage
Done" it's a house as big as a block as old
Maybe as Morgantown. It's not that it's necessarily
Haunted, the haunts came from up the block
There was a murder Andrea took to her man
With a hammer says "Cancer is the living Christ"
Within me. I was her babysitter.
House of proximities, soaked with it.
Over there, pry inside around back
There's a duck pond inside the house.
Story says owned by Mob.

The place isn't even gothic.
If Gothic went Gothic,
It might be this house.
No one enters or exits house.
The dealers steer clear
Of you when you are this big.
It's the I can't get you in my camera house.
If Clue was a real game,
Shocks of turquoise and red interiors
Imagine every single event that has taken place here.
This is what I meant by the 30,000 of it.

Hydra house
Hangs "T.B. Sheets"
Slate shingles influenza influential
Quaffs Maker's Mark
Crazy John mowed the lawn.
Draw near, John will ask you
"Where'd you get those spindly legs?"

Was a rich schizophrenic
Who lived in Hotel Morgan
Aka "Hot Organ" after the
Electric letters failed
To light the night.

How Old Is It?

1. <u>1766</u>

Tree did it look to witness Zackquill Morgan?
Washington detects the tree on land survey,
tomahawk had its rights, it call genocide,
Bounds White Avenue, antipodal addicts
Glare at the school behind it, smoking ganja
"Humbolt" meant killer. Looking backward, Faces
Facing forward – this twist was Canto Twenty.
Zack Morgan, he acted the same - "potential".
Prospect anticipates the outcome, leaves the
Tree surrounded. Stuck condition. Civil War is
Circular looking glass; its made of guns and
Cash and of industry. The ground it soaks the
Blood, the tree does not care. An energy that

Is Itself, unconditional condition

2. Letter Excerpt From my Great-Great-Grandfather to his Wife

(written by William Porter Wilkin
Captain, First West Virginia Cavalry
Annapolis, Md., July 31, 1863)

Dear Wife . . . .
On the 20th we landed in Richmond a little before daylight; and being tired
and weary I lay down in the street of the Confederate capitol and fell asleep,
when I dreamed I was engaged in a most desperate and bloody battle, I
thought we slew the rebels by the thousands, but still they pressed on with
increasing vigor and increasing recklessness of life. I fought with power and
strength that I thought were supernatural. I was half crazed with delight over
the terrible havoc I was making in their ranks when I was struck by a ball
and fell dead, as I thought, but still in my mind was active. I had many novel

reflections of which I have not the time to tell you, but I thought of the battle-field, with peculiar pleasure. I thought of my family and wondered how long it would be before I must pass over now. Finally, I thought, as I am in the land of spirits, I must begin to look around me and see what my doom is to be. So I gathered myself up, or rather was wafted along, I knew not whither; yet my motions were not involuntary — I had power to direct my course. Presently I came in sight of a place that excited my curiosity; it did not exactly answer Milton's description of hell, yet I thought it must be hell. But in order to be well assured of the place I jogged along till the sentinel at the gates halted me. I will not attempt to describe this sentry, suffice it to say he was the most perfect looking object of pain and anguish and suffering that imagination could picture. I ventured to inquire who he was, and what the place was that he was guarding. "I, sir, am the renowned Calhoun of South Carolina, and the first instigator of rebellion in the U. S., and this place sir, is a special hell, got up for the especial benefit of all traitors and rebels to the Government of the U. S., together with C. L. Vanllandigham, of Ohio, and his followers; and it is as much more miserable than the old original hell, as the original hell is more miserable than heaven. And with that, he uttered a piercing shriek, so full of woe, unutterable anguish, and despair, so hellish and infernal, that it startled me and I sprang to my feet and awoke, to laugh a good hearty laugh at the ludicrousness of my dream. Perhaps the rough usage we had been receiving from the rebels for some days past gave rise to the dream. At daylight we were marched through the streets and crammed in a large warehouse opposite Castle Thunder. One thousand of us were crowded into this place, the filthiest place I ever saw — and kept there till evening, when were marched out and over to Bell Island — Here we lay for three days on this sandbar, without any shelter to protect us from the scorching heat of the sun. During these days I was very sick and being thus exposed I suffered very much. On the 23rd we were loaded into stock cars and joyously started on our way to Chesapeake Bay for a truce. We landed in due time, as such a set of morale that I ever saw; some laughed, some shouted, and some even really cried with joy, when we came in sight of the flag-of-truce boat, and beheld the stars and stripes waving from her masthead. We were soon embarked and heading down the James River. Thence we proceeded up Chesapeake Bay to Annapolis where we landed on the 24th, and where we were soon rid of our old clothing and clad in garments new and clean and where rations were dealt out plentifully.

When I landed here I was very weak and what little flesh I had was all gone . . . . I think it very long since I heard from you, but hope in a few days to receive a letter from you. When you write again, you had better direct to the regiment, at Washington D.C., for I hope to be with the reg't. in a few days.

Yours as ever,
William Porter Wilkin

3. Chiasm

Over time tree go big. Can't look around it
Anymore. Tree gather history. Those on one
Side, not on the other, White Avenue occluded.
Dwarfs all, even "the house" looks small
In compare, that street sign's a joke.
Hide and seek, make out, down the street from Johnny's
Where Gretchen and I listened to Kasey Kasem
American Top Forty. Sometimes, dad, Elizabeth,
Rebecca, and I would try to encircle the trunk
With our hands held together. That reach is what lifts
You but you can't see you looking backward,
The jesusline needs the demon, engines run on flesh.

after Iñigo Manglano-Ovalle's always after (the glass house)

The van's normal load is usually nine per square yard. In Saurer vehicles, which are very spacious, maximum use of space is impossible, not because of any possible overload, but because loading to full capacity would affect the vehicle's stability. So reduction of the load space seems necessary. It must absolutely be reduced by a yard, instead of trying to solve the problem as hitherto, by reducing the number of pieces loaded. Besides, this extends the operating time, as the empty void must also be filled with carbon monoxide. On the other hand, if the load space is reduced, and the vehicle is packed solid, the operating time can be 10 considerably shortened. The manufacturers told us during a discussion that reducing the size of the van's rear would throw it badly off balance. The front axle, they claim, would be overloaded. In fact, the balance is automatically restored, because the merchandise aboard displays during the operation a natural tendency to rush to the rear doors, and is mainly 15 found lying there at the end of the operation. So the front axle is not overloaded. The lighting must be better protected than now. The lamps must be enclosed in a steel grid to prevent their being damaged. Lights could be eliminated, since they apparently are never used. However, it has been 20 observed that when the doors are shut, the load always presses hard against them [against the doors] as soon as darkness sets in. This is because the load naturally rushes toward the light when darkness sets in, which makes closing the doors difficult. Also, because of the alarming nature of darkness, screaming always occurs when the doors are closed. 25 It would therefore be useful to light the lamp before and during the first moments of the operation. For easy cleaning of the vehicle, there must be a sealed drain in the middle of the floor. The drainage hole's cover, eight to twelve inches in diameter, would be equipped with a slanting trap, so that fluid liquids can drain off during the operation. During cleaning, the drain can be used to evacuate large pieces of dirt. The aforementioned technical changes are to be made to vehicles in service only when they come in for repairs. As for the ten vehicles ordered from Saurer, they must be equipped with all innovations and 35 changes shown by use and experience to be necessary.' Claude Lanzmann, *Shoah: An Oral History of the Holocaust* (New York: Pantheon Books, 1985), 103-105.

we are only debating aftermath
after math after what
once was swept up
and kept as if transparent
if and only.

what?
a blanking repetition t
hat in its unblinking
"I'm the city of god against the pagans"
reinforced smasht skulls
with what —
once always after,
over and over
it's at the river
or the macbethy hands.

One is not one one is.
we arrived after celan got there.
always — even before there was,
was.

ever machinic transparent
we hold strung up hands
juiced and ravaged

                                           this little van of mine!

incalculable love irreplaceability
and fundament of reciprocity
after which both of us
come to the show a little bloody.
magic region of phase space where self-organizing effects are maximized, that is,
where spontaneous self-organization reaches a peak in complexity.

I tried to convince my family to go to Auschwitz for educational purposes.)
the idea of transparency,

the I can tell you truthfully's
glassed, bashed, head full of foam
we put on are headfoams and walk arm in fucking arm.
after this comes that and the carelessness
how I'm so sorry for ____.
a little cut up'
emoticon and gunface.
cleaned up
and back out.
rinse, repeat.
"do-overs."

Never, Noviodunum
     elle — *"I was born in Never,*
     I grew up in Never,
     I learned to read in Never,
     that's where I turned 20

     when you're in the cellar, Am I dead?

     youre dead.
useless swearing sewed up hands
swept and weeping,
   this jabby of legitimated,
              Eisenstein *this is the glass sky that I invented in Berlin*

   strung up gut factories already functioning equally
Taylor's disassembly lines of meat
hey Holocaust Chicago
prep meat talk to Upton Sinclair about that one.
     Afterwards I don't remember anymore.
     how long? how long? (eternity/

—I'm glad you grew your hair back!

You
for J.G.

I'm reading these poems
for somebody else,
Who may be me.
There is a tooth-calling
husked in print,
inverted awl eyes who
who can you hear?

I'm reading these poems
for somebody else.
Did you write them?
Taut skein day gauze
tightly tucked round
"the life." Underneath,
the manifest juts or
etches out our shapes.

I'm reading these poems
for someone else so the
scissors can cut cut the etched
up beings now animated
or, as so often is the case,
failed beings with cleft heart notes
or how war slices us into twos.

I'm reading these poems
for somebody else. They could be
graveyard sonatas, orchestral
arrangements. Celan understood this.
I'm reading these
poems in order to not yet die.
And casting dirt

from your slickened shovels,
carving up pa pa poetries,
the audience does dig it,
we get into it,
before the lights go off.

thought I told you the lights go off.
I'm reading these poems for some One
else. Who is writing them —
could that be
I'm writing these poems to you?
Are you writing these poems too?
How coy, how narcotic.
Some flood the doors
chanting chance not robotic
but left for luck's idea
sketched out here at the last
stop where you and I
may gather. If that's you.

Some declarative who,
with riches and magic tricks
with tricks and no riches.
Some declare and decide,
choose to slide writing these
nothings into sweet airs
that only we can see.
I'm reading these poems
for some body else,
so we may have nothing
you, me, the parlors
and everything I read
I did, to "strike a fancy"
which left what once was misery
with a cleft note

closing down, down.
let me read these sketches
in your part of town.

I said town, which is how that place
feels. something sent, not a square,
not a government or Citizen.
Ghost towns needle their
way or the way
you flex your back
but that is not what
catches me. I'm reading The
these your poems,
next to knife fight stories
and thrift shop
clasp the unclasped
or clapping at years.
You are not fungible,
revocable. This much I know
and burn. I'm deleting these
poems for someone else.
Are they less real?
Will this true the circumstance
of their occasion?

I'm not reading,
but noting the pace of your
foot and legs which fold and
tap swift and slow erratic
there is nothing as if
and nothing as
beautiful as this love.
How could they be?
Impeachable consciousness, an

endless interrogation would not
produce an answer that was not
already there. bodies. poems.
the between. There's something in
the grammar I do not understand,
yet I'm to follow its Law.

I'm writing this poem to everyone else
an adhesion of animal
and all-power. Is it corporeal?
I'm watching these poems walk in
from the storm.
every one's delicate.
Might this prove harm we seek to avoid?
We look at each other and do not know.
I asked what Celan would do to live through
the night, not in order to die. Am I orchestrating?
Or subtract the Mathematical fringe distant gaze
of the Retributive Hateful Gods.
There is nothing as-if, nothing as beautiful —
Being's grammar
spelled out by someone else, by It.
If I walk, the wreckage multiplies.
To feel the new carved out of us
or "us" itself. "blind swipe of the pruner
and his knife, busy round the tree of life."

*

somebody slap me
I'm reading the real reeling
these poems
This one's a film too
in reel time.
Its words are brine,

some horses black under
fundaments of Earth. Trample hyacinth petal.
Were you writing from a meadow?

I think I should like the meadow,
as was schooled and thought it blood.
You're carving some poems
somewhere else, cavern
that this hermetic design cannot shadow
but shine
Kore.

without, but with a certain uncertain meter
these poems. this love. this time.
not just a poem
or anyone
or else
ever
or again.

Abuse, Survive, Love

1.

Abused and survive. It was like when I was, wasn't.
I was younger, smaller.
Nor is it like when
she nearly died after her husband
till she nearly died. She ignored all counsel
And tried to dream it away with little clear bottles
Of Narcotix. Maybe it was when ___ got like
Hit in the face   cast iron skillet.
Maybe. I don't know what goes on I can't make heads or tails of
How nature is charged with doling out these blows.
I also tried to find an answer to the next and next crime or
What happened after to her. I know our addresses,
Have no clue where we are at though. We talk whenever
Our parents' lives are in danger, which is more often these days.

2.

Ask Void — for answer.
Convex, its teeth all Chatter.
Convey, pitched to the Other.
What humans don't hear.

3.

Then You.
Inversion of all of the above
Which gives me ears to hear.
How happen?
Snippet of a flock
Arcs and arches over lover
Springs and clover.

How is it, so fortunate?

So wild, strange, inimitable.
And perfectly tune the day
And your tones, also perfected.
The moon being lunar, alone,
Is lunatic.
I dote and dote and dote!

You are verse fantastic
And the making of the verse
And that which made the making of the verse.
You drive hearses in reverse
All subtraction from You is hearsay.

Once, well more than, but once
I got all mathematical and tried to calculate.
Everything about you is incalculable.
How could anyone speak to You
Of sizes? Does not compute.
Come closer again that we might find
Each other and leave subtraction in dust.
(I read your cousin in Song of Songs the other day.)

Everything I say is silenced in awe of it.
But, I could say the perfection of your neck
And would not be wrong.
I will say the perfection of your neck and am not wrong.
I say the perfection of your neck and am not wrong.
You. Emily said 'I held my spirit to the glass/to prove it possibler'.
All that you say, think, feel, even your vicious wit,
Even that, all of you, all of your body, not one iota less pulled
My spirit in and then, possibler.
Every move its reversal.
Of all that is or is not, indelible.
Behind each cloud, "stintless stars"

And who would be
Goddess for Each of These?
I have imagined much but all
I've seen, heard, tasted, touched —
Only you, now I finally know Love.
The Burning is Complete
And thus, growing day by day,
Amaze.
But Charlie nature took a leap that day
And came to the river's poison floors
I got all jittery and wisht the invert
Shadow state Hobbesld monster
Stript and stripper, dead blues monster
Gript and giffy with Pride
Prickles his needle armor
Or at least amor,
But no, lickety-split. Done in
At the start of it his silly invert
Played the part issuing stays of execution
To enact the next idea, ownership of death.

Dear Jason, The slide show didn't matter
To them. I could tell by the way they kept their
Profiles; courage boys, God fearing.
Fish face hidden sweaty hotel mercury moons
And tectonic Mandelbrot sweats
(Mohammed saw the moon splitting)
a Goyan dream
of all the fuckings
The Gideon has ever seen.

A Sort of Homecoming

for Jacob Knabb

This skin huffs
And bounds, it slept
Thru spent and caustic
Skoal kitchen
Grist y bourbon
Maple buckwheat table.

"We" and chitterings
unglued from their seams,
these birds differ
so it's cast iron
decision sterny beer
man "it's afternoon
somewheres."

And also of the flocks
Who spend 430 am
Riffing inverted with
Bats. Sonar v lunar
Look at what rifles
A chimney. He clean
With underwear getup
Outsides spill
Animals griddled with sonic
Attack.

*

— Once. Mourns
for fitful rivers
thought was father.

Bit by bit
It washes up cadavers.

Who unsees the
Hit laid down
Gouges mountains,
Who done scored
That last one
And black lung blues?

*

Shit-kicker.
He huff the same
Casting dirties
(without but also)
with
Dr. Basement
familial development
in roach in casts
His guts speared
Not with tomahawk
But them other
cirrhotic gaze trenches.

Everything about you is perfect,
so how come you hate yourself?
Not that don't I so understand,
your hand is damaged,
dealt from what once were napalm
card kits. Now punched in, a toothless
abode and adobe. hi skin sloven
skool crimi. hiss watch your death
from inside how your jesus liver stains
looped for fun 1975, you know, herpes disco
queens now inside you with little charts
string of joynts, "pure automatic functioning" (arendt 1958)
"the bloom is off the rose" (hagerty 2007)
hey sucker is ok man, every day
flowers forth from the chance to wipe it clean.
Enigmatic bondage splits up the hours,
body rock/rot God's' Great Gospel
Dawning holey punch in for a while
tell it to john brown
the significance, how you were an audiophile.

ologies

About which there was spades
Then laughter. He be made of angles,
Cuts across with time some marble
Slabs effervesce from cradle
He thought of an angel
With every desperate stab.
To avoid the hanging tree.
You could see
slew of you
That one dream of
an architecture to prove.
This wasn't you —
It's pure application.
A techno contempt
For what wasn't
Is the making
It's just an old fashioned
o deliberate hanging
How many of you hang you?
To stave silence
With a certain type

Blasphemous Temple

I.

blasphemous temple.
both from the orders
· and the orders' bridges.

he thot he had to thing
with every story of kindness.

II.

storied arm, with its dotted
explanations "had to keep them
separate because I love them both"
and other pits.

This was because of it.
Ventricle and outside
the arms flapping.
A thudded twitch
in tundra.
dribs of it, glistering.

III.

a kind of temple,
this pit
(hello damaged
boy sunset room.)
where he comes in
its okay it's got prayerrrs
n cherubim so it's protected
look at the safe let's open
the safe together it's like a
game let's cram for the safe
the safe is so fun and secrete
and . . . creepy Jesus stains
undulate under
dancing light or catastrophic logic
it's an eyecloser with the little
squinty floater particles skipping
around and tracers on
every faithful grunt into the maw.

IV.

Storied order of the Faithful Bridges
The secret blessing of a Flapper
from Wisconsin with curly fingers
and an eye on Turner.
Dribbing paint in pangs
from thudded tundra,
snowy castigations
long before CAT scans
(there's something wrong with you walks in again)
and promenade of Oaks
heave wave.
hand in the pit
warmed the earth
and the humans
surrounding it
save for infinitesimal rooms
where they did things
too with Christ and ham radio.

arms

he looked at me and said,
"yer a phlebotomist's fantasy."

who did. and jabs and stills
a boister faster than liquor.

"I can't help it, when I go down
the street I check everyone out

not checking out checking out,
sayin to myseff oo I can get him right there!

and that, that one would be tuff."
having blown out my left arm

I seemed fantastical,
from the right.

hospitals

Every play matters now
O don't look so frightened
Don't you get puffed up yet
Cuz I know this is nothing new,
And o the dew is wet under your palms
As only pawns will go there with you
And these are those with whom you
Surround. As this gets gathered with that,
Stabby of hillside. That annoying pauper's
Graveyard don't tell but I sware I saw
One palm wave through the soft dirt.

I hope you under stand that I need to cut off
My fingers and fangs for you,
In honor and respectfully. Nothing you
Say or do can uncanny convince me
Which is why I'm tied down at the moment
With those little medics moving in
And the Call of the Sirens
Splits the scarlet night in half
O this is not how I scripted
the incident to end.

I.

She thinks the monkey's bad luck because
of all the Institutions it's seen.
A curious curious George hooked to my hoodie,
with arguably racialized, inappropriate lips
curling out to smile and greet the staff
as I ask for the nth time why no release
or where is Albeheary? By now,
anything may well prove to be true,
which, of course, is insane.

II.

Sometimes I lose it. If I can't wear it,
When I'm on the outside, the backpack
Or higgly pocket. Little higgly pigglies
Tearing at the tongue. Speak to me.
Who, art? Thinning. More vodka.
This time Lakeshore third floor,
My DTs I can't dial. The kindest black
Trans/guy who did my dialing for me.
Others tore their hair out or hanged themselves.

My roomie he collapsed his lung
Eleven times. This is his last trip to the place.
Eventual. Even. They moved me I got the same roommate
Last New Year's as the one before.
The shakes are permanent.
The stain all the more so, like nothing.
Inside, a perpetual processing. This is prisoning.
Ever emotion's measured. "wrong" (with you)
This isn't as or like anything. Outside, I just want back in.

III.

At one point, there was something to it.
As when he found a hernia on me in the tub
And suddenly, "operation." Herr Doctor.
Then hospital at five years old and a Curious
Curious George story. How he went too.
Or windup Campbell's Soup.
Of course he slept there, for solace. For comfort.
Night rounds. Book lernt animal instinct.
Aping compassion. Inappropriate lips. The old testament wronged.

Wait Til All The Bees Are Gone

wait til all the bees are gone,
your laughing chastise excludes
its own, inverted, like a hole
that's completely hole. entire
stars go through this. I go through
this, with and for you but am
no more, "cardiac," fortune
of blood, freely flowing it's
abundants, recognize that
\ exlectricity. profuse
After the storm, the divine
dividing minds separate
the branches and step outside.
Against it all, there's still a
glance and as such it's only
embrace charged with matter.
Stilled by the waiting as
if the news was negative.
Or would be. Fear scares itself,
recharges and blasts sharper
animals from their bones. Large
birthing blast blackened by blood,
in charge of nothing. Which is
not, of course, what will be.